Bulletin Board-ers

Two Thousand Statements
for
Bulletins
Sign Boards
Posters and Bulletin Boards
Sermon Titles
Wall Hangings

Larry Eisenberg

CSS Publishing Company, Inc., Lima, Ohio

BULLETIN BOARD-ERS

Reprinted 2002

Copyright © 1973 by
CSS Publishing Company, Inc.
Lima, Ohio
Second Printing 1984
Third Printing 1984
Fourth Printing 1989

All rights reserved. No part of this publication may be reproduced in any manner whatsoever without the prior permission of the publisher, except in the case of brief quotations embodied in critical articles and reviews. Inquiries should be addressed to: Permissions, CSS Publishing Company, Inc., P.O. Box 4503, Lima, Ohio 45802-4503.

For more information about CSS Publishing Company resources, visit our website at www.csspub.com or e-mail us at custserv@csspub.com or call (800) 241-4056.

ISBN 0-89536-017-9   PRINTED IN U.S.A.

TABLE OF CONTENTS

Introduction	5
General Quotes	11
Punchy Quotes	23
Quotes About God	33
Quotes About Jesus	37
Faith, Hope, Love	41
Love	43
Christian Service	45
Healing	47
Sin, Salvation	49
Christian	51
Bible	53
Dealing With The Negatives	55
Prayer	57
Quotes About "You"	59
Youth	63
The Seasons	65
People, Friends	67
Being Critical	69
Forgiveness	71
Church	73
Affirmations	75
Home, Marriage	77

Worry, Hate, Fear, Suffering, Pride	79
Succeed, Fail, Struggle	81
Optimist	83
Truth	85
Enthusiasm	87
Happiness, Joy	89
Kindness	91
Free	93

Welcome to the "Church Bulletin Board Club!" Who are we? We're enthusiasts who value the public ministry enough to erect and use a signboard beamed at the needs of the community. It takes time, but it's a rewarding ministry. We can even get excited about it!

I stumbled into the ministry. We had an old signboard, and I talked Ginny Hill into changing it daily with spiritual or pithy sayings. Since people could hardly see the board, Dan Varsvary became interested in helping us have a better one. He made a substantial contribution toward a new double-faced sign in the church yard on Highway 23. We recognized that as many as 10,000 people a day could see it, here in Wise, Virginia.

We found what we wanted in a JONESIGN, made by a consecrated layman, D. L. Jones, who fabricated it in his Northside Tin Shop, 340 Frazier Avenue, Chattanooga, Tennessee 37405, for about half the cost of other signs. His pastor, Bill Horner, had helped him with the design. Mr. Jones furnished us with original quotations to use on the signboard.

It wasn't long before we discovered that we had a great ministry to people in all walks of life. "The sign" became lunch table conversation at The Inn. Students at Clinch Valley College would come to see what was on our sign. Humble, even ragged people would tell us what the sign meant to them.

KEEPING IT INTERESTING

We discovered quickly its preaching possibilities, but recognized as quickly that to keep people looking we had to alternate some "sharp" sayings. As I evaluated its effect, I decided that its functions somewhat paralleled the special rooms in the church itself. We have the sanctuary for worship and inspiration and comfort; the classrooms for teaching, and the fellowship hall and kitchen for food and fun. So with the sign!

Therefore, I have tried to vary greatly what our sign carries. We try to appeal to the settled church crowd, but also the high school crowd and the college group, occasionally the offbeat youth crowd, the person with limited education, and on occasion people with rich vocabularies. We've been "funny" and "cute," but we also haven't hesitated to "preach" and to call for Christian decision and deeply-dedicated Christian living.

One special development has been a ministry to the bereaved. We're in a small town and when we know of a bereavement and feel that the person may read the sign, we use quotations to minister to them for perhaps 2-4 days. We like to use the sign as a Community Bulletin Board, since ours is in the most public place in town. We've announced concerts, school events, and game scores, and have publicized happenings in churches other than our own.

USING A SERIES

The "series" is a live possibility, using a running theme for several days ... or question one day and answer another, etc. We have made some seasonal use of the Board at Christmas, Easter, Thanksgiving.

MAKE YOUR OWN

People have asked, "How did you get all those quotations?" From every kind of source imaginable.

From the Bible ... from popular magazines like *Reader's Digest* and *Sunshine Magazines* ... humor books, speakers' books, popular psychology ... the books that ministers read for their own purposes. I put an "S" for "sign" in the margin when I find a good quotation, and copy it out later. Members of our church have occasionally furnished them to us, and enjoy seeing their contribution on the board. It's great fun to discover new ones, especially if they have a sharp ring to them!

We're irregular about changing the board, but try to do it about every day or three times a week. This takes time, but we feel that it is abundantly worth it. I believe it has helped to change the image of the church from a reserved, staid image to a much warmer one.

SOME OTHER USES OF THIS MATERIAL

We've tried to reduce the quotations to lines that will fit a sign needing not more than 21 characters, 3 lines. But there are other uses than for signs.

1. POSTERS or WALL HANGINGS. Youth or some other group in the church might make a series of posters or felt banners using some of this material.

2. CHURCH BULLETINS. Use them for "bulletin liners." Or in news sheets.

3. MEMORIZE SOME for conversation purposes.

4. USE in sermons and other messages, restating if needed.

5. SOME OF THE QUOTATIONS came from those used by leaders of small groups.

RESOURCES

Let us share some references with you.

THE BIBLE. We've used the King James, The Living Bible, Phillips' Translation mostly.

QUOTATION BOOKS. We've especially liked Paul Holdcraft's *Minute Messages for Church Calendars and Bulletin Boards* (Abingdon Press, Nashville), Eleanor Doan's *The Speaker's Sourcebook* (Zondervan), and Jim Hefley's *The Sourcebook Of Humor* (Zondervan).

THE AMERICAN BIBLE SOCIETY has two beautiful sets of posters for the wall and possibly bulletin boards, on Love and Joy. They are 18 x 30 inches in florescent colors. Each set of five is about $3.50. American Bible Society, Box 5656, Grand Central Station, New York 10017.

I've found certain writers using a "bulletin board" style of expressing themselves. Cecil G. Osborne does it well in *The Art Of Understanding Yourself* and *The Art Of Understanding Your Mate* (both Zondervan Publishing). I also have found Dr. George W. Crane doing it in *Guidebook For Counseling* (Hopkins Syndicate, Inc., 520 N. Michigan Avenue, Chicago, Illinois). Keith Miller's *Taste Of New Wine* and *Second Look* (Word Publishing, Waco, Texas) and Leander Keck's *Mandate To Witness* (Judson Press, Valley Forge, Pennsylvania) helped us, as did Dr. Earl A. Loomis' *The Self In Pilgrimage* (Harper & Row), and Stephen Neill's *Creative Tension* (Edinburgh House Press, London). Norman Vincent Peale, *Enthusiasm Makes The Difference* (Guideposts, Carmel, New York). E. Stanley Jones' books from Abingdon Press like *Abundant Living* use bulletin board type phrases. You sort of develop a mind for it.

AND IN CONCLUSION ...

We want to thank our members and other people in Wise, Virginia, who have shared "boarders" with us ... Pat Garrett and Helen Eisenberg for helping get the material together ... Geneva Stallard, Jim Roberson, Tom Hill, Preston Boggs, Bill Horner, George Dunbar, Plato, Socrates, Abe Lincoln, and all the rest ... and a very special thanks to Wesley T. Runk of CSS Publishing Company, for offering so graciously to make these Boarders available to you.

Larry Eisenberg
Trinity United Methodist Church
Wise, Virginia
September 29, 1972

I have arranged these loosely into categories, but as you can see quickly, some will fit more than one category.

First there will be some "punchy, eye-catching" quotes, then some more general ones and finaly some labeled by categories. Mix 'em up! And gather your own!

GENERAL QUOTES

* God gave two hands — one for him, one for fellow man
* Daily prayers lessen daily cares
* The strong must help the weak
* God is the infinity of good
* When you can't face existence alone, turn to a higher power
* Today — first things first!
* Happiness is loving God
* Happiness is loving your neighbor as yourself!
* Happiness is truly loving yourself
* It takes more courage to repent than to keep on sinning!
* God rewards not success but faithfulness
* "Little" is much when God is in it!
* If God is for us, who can be against us?
* Arguing often displays our ignorance!
* The courageous go forward in spite of their fears
* Real courage only holds on five minutes longer
* Maturity is bearing injustice without getting even
* "Be anxious for nothing"
* If you want one thing, ask God for another, you get chaos
* Vision sees through a problem — courage sees it through
* We're incapable of accepting God's love until we repent
* Money can provide nearly everything but happiness
* God measures loyalty by service
* Look what Jesus did with a towel!
* Fasting has power to cleanse body, mind, and spirit
* Give peace a chance!
* Today — send our many kindly thoughts
* "Our business is to do what lies clearly at hand." — Carlyle
* Pride is the mother of self-pity
* "Every reform was once a private opinion." — Emerson
* Today — try giving people a good listening-to!
* The truly great are seldom conformists
* People are the only animals eating themselves to death
* The purpose of all life is growth
* Are you knifing the one who carries you on his back?

* You can't go on being a good egg — you hatch or go bad!
* Love is great, brothers and sisters, pass it on!
* Man tends to symbolize and worship the symbol
* We act about life the way we talk about it!
* If you can smile in the mirror, there's hope!
* A reversal is an incident, not a disaster!
* Democracy says, "You are equal to me." — James R. Lowell
* Lust for anything says: "I must have it at once!"
* You master yourself when you master your temper!
* To be exactly opposite is also a form of imitation
* Tackle today that hard thing you've been avoiding
* "I have never known an alcoholic not running from self." — Mann
* When we get men of vision, we call them "visionary"
* In the concert of nations, each still sings a different key
* "Anger is a stone cast in a wasp's nest." — Proverbs
* True nobility is being superior to your former self
* A learned man carries his wealth with him
* "The first product of self-knowledge is humility." — O'Connor
* "Thirst after gold is worse than thirst after water." — Proverb
* The first screw to loosen controls the tongue
* You can't go back — time is a one-way stream
* "An angry wise man ceases to be wise." — The Talmud
* Every person has a right to die with dignity
* Commit this day to God and really get going!
* Man cannot lift himself by his own bootstraps
* Everybody needs a deep spiritual experience
* "As a man thinks in his heart, so is he."
* Gratitude is the most exquisite form of courtesy
* Treat others as you think God would treat them
* No power but you continues bad habits
* "Anger is always a defense against fear." — Stella Mann
* Candles exhaust themselves in giving light
* Insults, like bad coins, need not be taken
* "Life is to grow surely and safely toward God." — Mann
* Greatness lies in the right use of strength
* To get respect, act respectably

* Blessed be this day to you and yours!
* A smile: The magic language that even a baby understands
* Too often we seek justice just for us
* Integrity comes from years of patient well-doing
* Attitude more than aptitude, determines success
* Every person has some power to change himself
* Somebody today needs a compliment from you
* Count your blessings, name them one by one
* Pearl Bailey: "When you wear a label, 'I am' you're not!"
* A baby is God's opinion that the world should go on!
* Anger is a wind blowing out the lamp of the mind
* "Criminality is never inherited." — Dr. G. W. Crane
* "Find sermons in stones, good in everything"
* An expert keeps his mouth shut when not sure of right answers
* If you can't be a star in the sky, be a lamp!
* A smile is a light in the window of your soul
* Illusion: That there'll be more time tomorrow!
* Memory can be too comfortable a shelter!
* Small boy in pool of sunlight: "I'm in the smile of God!"
* Self is the unjolly giant!
* Finally you can't "beat the game" and cheat the universe
* The poorest man is one with nothing but money.
* We need deeply to belong to a united mankind!
* "Power over life needs to be balanced by reverence for life." — Ann Lindbergh
* To avoid criticism: Do nothing, say nothing, be nothing!
* Peacemakers don't say: "The trouble with you is ..."
* There is really no right way to do a wrong thing
* "Let justice roll down like a mighty stream!"
* "Saints" are the men the light shines through!
* Our spirits are willing but the metabolism is weak!
* Empty hearts, not empty pockets, hold us back
* A friend is one who lets you be fully yourself
* Worse than quitting — being afraid to begin!
* "I don't have time" doesn't state fact but intent
* A friend is a present you give yourself
* Good habits take effort — bad ones little

* All colors together make white light
* "I always compromise except when I know I'm right!"
* "We're glad you came" — Note: Knoxville has this as a town slogan
* We're not to endure life but to master it
* "Yes, but ..."
* In every problem are the seeds of its solution
* Honesty is the backbone of civilization
* It's hard to be both real friend and flatterer
* In quietness and confidence shall be your strength
* "The mind is only right when at peace with itself." — Seneca
* May you live all the days of your life
* Truly intelligent people are truly modest
* "The thornbush by the wayside is a flame with the glory of God"
* "Anger manages everything badly." — Statius
* You draw from the bank of life what you deposit
* It's no tribute to forefathers to camp where they fell!
* Anger always has a reason — seldom a good one
* "Do it now — you'll then have time for something else!"
* Blessed are the peacemakers — sons of God!
* Much of the world's work is done by those who don't feel good!
* We are entering the cage of universal human history
* Some lives have the radiance of a snuffed-out candle!
* It's one thing to praise discipline, another to submit!
* This too shall pass!
* People respond more to how we feel than what we say!
* The proud are not truly happy!
* The worthwhile is often small
* When a child asks questions, you see how little you know!
* The worst boss is a bad habit
* War is the fruit of man's transgressing God's moral law
* Without fire, religion is dead ashes!
* What you ought to do, you can do!
* "Convince a man, persuade a woman"
* "A sunset is heaven's gate left ajar"

* Character is the ability to ignore an insult
* Life is not a fate but a privilege
* Blessed are those who give up arguments for the sake of peace
* Our true willing controls our acts
* Tension makes a string make music
* Religion is a way of looking at everything
* When good men do nothing, evil triumphs
* "Secret Service Christians" only show themselves when safe
* Can anyone conquer the dulling effect of luxury?
* "A wholesome tongue is a tree of life" — Proverbs 15:4
* "The sweetness of the orange is in the stem" — African saying
* To lighten life's load, lift the weight from someone else's back
* "Count each day as a separate life." — Seneca
* No one lives who is as good as he knows to be!
* To the impure all are impure!
* We do little worth doing by accident!
* The revolutionaries of history have been prisoners
* Keep young while growing old!
* Christians are not guaranteed tensionless peace!
* Be led by dreams, not pushed by problems!
* Learn from your successes!
* It's hard for a free fish to understand a hooked one!
* Intelligence is the ability to learn how to learn
* "If everybody were just like me, what a world!"
* Living involves tearing up one rough draft after another
* With every problem there is the seed of greater benefit
* Are you a self-holic?
* Human rights are based upon human dignity
* The handcuffs to the new are custom and tradition
* Child: "Do we pray at night to get the cheaper rate?"
* We treat God's world as if there's a spare in the trunk
* Everyone dies — but not everyone lives!
* Constant renewal comes from constant thanksgiving
* Fresh mountain brooks pass on what they receive
* Death is not a "period" but a semicolon in life
* The soul is your spiritual radar
* With perfect truth life takes on a new meaning

* Even a short life is long enough to do some good!
* Hindsight shows what foresight could have prevented!
* Live as if this were your last day on earth!
* Don't complain that days are few but act like they're endless!
* Little lives are tamed by misfortunes
* Give away smiles today — free!
* The cross is written at the very heart of the universe
* Character is shown by the criticism you forgive
* When there's nothing to be thankful for, you've hit bottom!
* "Our disease is our brokenness." — Tillich
* Where there is hatred, try showing love!
* The upward way usually isn't the easy one
* Think a good day, thank a good day, pray a good day
* "Wrong thinking has devastating physical effects." — Tournier
* The majority of us belong to some minority group!
* Good tends to evaporate when we make it absolute
* If you seek perfect friends, you'll never find them
* Originality is a pair of fresh eyes
* Today: Say what you mean and mean what you say!
* Like some ovens, some heat up but seldom cook!
* A common problem: Living tomorrow's life today!
* Smile! God loves you!
* What does a candle lose by lighting another?
* Power corrupts the few, weakness the many
* "If you want a great quality, act as if you have it" — James
* Live and help live!
* Today — do the duty that lies nearest
* The mountain brook is never still
* Fight the good fight with all your might!
* "Sensible people harmonize their differences." — Allen
* It's not right to do less than your best
* A brook without rocks has no song
* The faithful in hard places can be trusted in high places
* Water's deep, sky's high. Makes you stop and wonder why. — Pat
* Nature to be commanded must be obeyed
* Who says you can't?

* "Life's no brief candle — it's a splendid torch!" — G. B. Shaw
* "Put a song in the heart of every word you speak!" — Mann
* We live in deeds, not years!
* Self-centeredness doth a prison make!
* Things you see in others are prevalent in thee!
* A good example is the best sermon
* You can teach an old dog new tricks!
* "Everywhere I go, I go too, and spoil everything." — Hoffenstein
* Only the day dawns to which we are awake!
* Today: Take some time for solid meditation!
* True piety enables you to forgive
* Today: Put the best construction on every person and action
* The weight of a full day's load would break any bridge!
* Little people talk most — big people listen most
* "Be still and know" then "get up and go!"
* "Only the young die good!" — Oliver Herford
* Christianity is not a theory — it is a life!
* The mature can take undeserved blame!
* Specialize in doing what you can't!
* "Character" is to remove your enemies by praising them
* "Having the right to do it" doesn't mean it's right to do it!
* You can get much done if you don't care who gets credit!
* "There are no gains without pains!" — Franklin
* It's the inner values that live forever!
* "All things are possible to him who truly believes"
* A seed must fall into the earth and die to bring fruit
* We make a good future by right use of the present
* He who is not going forward is going backward!
* All great souls are realists!
* Don't slump!
* "The most fundamental drive is for meaning in life." — Franklin
* Some things are so important they're worth doing badly!
* Lincoln's mother: "Abe, be somebody."
* Make the golden rule your daily rule!
* No one lives or dies of himself alone
* Bad labels can destroy the best of men
* If this were judgment day, how would you do?

* There are false values in the kingdom of thingdom
* No, we're not all going to the same place!
* Do your best with what you've got where you are!
* The best tranquilizer is a clear conscience
* "Man must end war or war will end man." — John Kennedy
* Anticipation is a magnifying glass for the emotions
* With nature and men — we reap what we sow!
* Ever hear of someone losing a job for not drinking?
* Today is ready cash — spend it wisely!
* Don't accept humdrum life without a fight!
* To be unhappy, focus on your woes!
* Are you drinking or gargling at the fount of knowledge?
* For a higher way of life, look up!
* "To sleep well lie not with enmity in thy heart."
* Acting "cool" is often an evasion of life
* The glory of the free is to transmit this to their children
* Man cannot live by brain alone!
* Only thing improved by anger is arch on cat's back!
* Those who believe can create "pools of faith"
* You're never too busy to attend your own funeral!
* You don't know yourself until you deny yourself!
* To be preserved, talents must be invested
* The resurrection transforms believers into brothers
* The kingdom is now!
* Only a mediocre person is always at his best!
* "Gracious uncertainty" is the mark of the spiritual life
* The "peace of the world" is incomplete and shallow
* Self-hate isn't virtuous — it's wrong!
* "The unexamined life is not worth living." — Socrates
* Think people up, not down!
* "Integrity" is loyal toward inner truth
* Leaving the garden, Adam said, "This is age of transition."
* A bootless man can't lift himself by his own bootstraps
* There are not hopeless situations, only hopeless men!
* You don't get experience for nothing!
* The seed you keep digging up doesn't grow
* The medium is the message — our words and lives are together

* A horse can't kick while he's pulling!
* "History teaches that man learns nothing from history." — Hegel
* "Badness is goodness dammed up." — Dr. Earl Loomis
* The restless change labels on empty bottles
* "Where your treasure is, there is your heart also"
* "Lord, keep me sweet — a sour person is a work of the devil!"
* Dialogue can't take the place of decision
* The neglected opportunity won't come back!
* The secret of being boring is to tell everything
* "We know truth both by reason and by the heart." — Pascal
* Go anywhere, if it's forward for you
* Don't be a "half-a-minder"
* It is a threat to society when adults stop learning
* "Right" brings responsibilities
* The library is one of our most democratic places
* Imagination is the secret reservoir of riches of the race
* Diplomat: One who can put in his own oar and not rock the boat!
* Today: Think in terms of miracles!
* "Often man does not die — he kills himself!" — Tournier
* Today: Let your talk match your walk!
* Fortune unmasks people
* Progress is applied imagination
* All men are islands! Bridge builders needed!
* A music teacher told Caruso his voice was like wind in shutters!
* Religion is a risk!
* "Be strong and of good course — be not afraid!"
* What about encouraging others all day today?
* Wisdom is being aware of your own follies
* You're not a failure until satisfied with being one
* "Private religion" is a painter with empty canvas
* Defeat isn't so bitter if you don't swallow it!
* Maturity is going from egocentricity to sociocentricity!
* Maturity is going from self-centered life to others-centered life!
* You are important to God in his scheme of things!
* Expect great things from God

* Attempt great things for God
* No man is honest until he is honest with God
* In God we trust?
* God never waits for the multitudes
* God in second place is not God to you
* God is eternal
* God is more than a superhuman waiting to grant us favors
* God is equally available to saint and sinner
* God is the same, yesterday, today, and forever
* God wants more to redeem than to punish
* Although uncertain of the next step we are certain of God
* God wants a social structure where men live in freedom
* God gives in superabundance
* God calls the whole person — vocation and all!
* God will restore, establish, and strengthen you!
* God can use distress to bring the "vision splendid"
* The knowledge of God is far from the love of him
* You enjoy new life because God became a human being
* God is now here!
* What evidence could you give that there is really God?
* God has made of one blood the people of earth.
* Don't fret because of evildoers — delight in God!
* Not everything in the name of God is the word of God
* "Create in me a clean heart, O God!"
* There's romance in serving the one who controls the universe
* The God of all creatures cares for you!
* Trust God with tomorrow — help somebody today!
* God, help me to see good things in unexpected places!
* God can speak all 2,000 human languages!
* Thank God for problems!
* All our fresh springs are in God!
* God's love accepts, forgives, and endures all things
* Bless the Lord at all times!
* With God you can't stay neutral!
* "Give thanks to the Lord — His mercy endures forever!"
* God loves us in spite of our foolishness!
* God wants not so much ability as usability!

* What I place in God's hands I still possess!
* Today is God's — tomorrow will be God's
* Away from God we eat spiritual husks
* God's resources are never exhausted!
* The more we decrease the more God can increase
* Make regular payments on your debt to God!
* God trusts his big ideas to the unafraid
* God will fill every need from his riches
* All things are possible with God!
* You can never be outside God's love and care
* God wins when we accept the riches of his kingdom
* God goes beyond people's faces to their hearts
* If God should refuse us, what's to become of us?
* Turn the corner! God is there, waiting for you!
* God never comes to an end!
* Love God with all your heart, soul, mind, and strength!
* God works in his own way and his own time
* God can't give his best things to the dishonest
* God is not an elective — you're for him or against him!
* Democracy is based on the idea of man as a child of God
* God is where the hurt is!
* God promises safe landing but not calm passage — Bulgarian Proverb
* When God says, "Do it," do it!
* Man, the highest of creation, should show forth God!
* Did you thank God today?
* This is a house of worship. Welcome!
* Don't point a finger — Hold out a hand
* Please be patient — God isn't finished with me yet!
* Epitaph: "He lit many fires in cold rooms"
* "Open for business on highest authority"
* Not failure, but low aim, is wrong!
* When it comes to giving, some stop at nothing!
* Many of your ailments could be cured here!
* Every new day offers a new beginning!
* Redemption center — no stamps needed
* What will you do with what you have left?

* Faultfinders seldom find anything else!
* (On a hot day) So you think it's hot here!
* Satan trembles when he sees weakest saint upon his knees!
* The temptation to laziness never grows old!
* Nothing is more costly or futile than vengeance
* Blowing out another's light doesn't make yours brighter
* The truth only hurts when it ought to!
* Not only cars are recalled by the maker
* Few get dizzy from doing good turns!
* Joy is not in things but in us!
* Worry is interest paid before it is due
* Speaking kindly does not hurt the tongue

"PUNCHY" QUOTES

* There's always free cheese in mousetraps
* For peace of mind resign as general manager of the universe
* To be thought wise, keep your mouth shut
* "Almost right" is still wrong!
* Old age isn't so bad when you think of the alternative
* Even after they come in, some keep knocking!
* The unmapped country is largely within us
* We fall the way we lean
* Tack — getting fleece from the flock without a flinch
* If "it goes without saying," let it go!
* 'Tisn't hard to pick out the best people — they'll help you!
* God doesn't let his regular customers down
* The oil can is mightier than the sword!
* "If you scatter thorns, don't go barefoot." — Ben Franklin
* In covering the subject, don't smother it!
* You can tell a person's ideals from his checkbook
* A wise navigator carries more ballast than sail
* You have to be little to belittle
* Electricity is improbable — we did so long without it!
* The seed you keep digging up doesn't grow
* To err is human, to admit it is not!
* Note: Your liver reacts to the state of your mind!
* Dedicated ignorance gets you nowhere
* Prejudice: Being down on what you're not up on
* "Ve get too soon oldt undt too late smart" — Pennsylvania Dutch saying
* There are no permanent victories in a moral universe
* It's easier to restrain a fanatic than revive a corpse!
* The future arrives here sooner than it used to!
* Whale advice: "The less spouting off you do, the better!"
* The world owes you a living, but you must work to collect it!
* Things aren't like they used to be, including you!
* You only drown from staying in the water!
* Adam and Eve had a third son who stayed out of trouble
* White lies can lead to color blindness

* How can you trust God with your immortal soul and not with 10¢?
* Some people's ideas are sound — all sound!
* These will be the good old days in 2022!
* When opportunity knocks, would you complain of noise?
* "Kind words won't wear out the tongue" — Danish saying
* It's hard to see the picture when you're inside the frame
* Whatever your lot in life, build something on it!
* Opportunities look bigger going than coming
* You can't spray perfume around without getting some on yourself!
* In France, even the little children speak French!
* Few gardens have only flowers!
* Have you sent ahead the first payment on your harp?
* A dog has friends — he wags tail not tongue!
* To become wise, note what happens when you're not!
* For free publicity, do something stupid in public
* Our egos often have "20-20 I sight"
* Fortune unmasks people
* "Do right! It will gratify some, astonish the rest!" — Mark Twain
* Much of God's work is done by those who don't feel good!
* We seldom stumble on something good sitting down!
* Neither skunks nor turtles solve problems best
* Stretching the truth doesn't make it last longer!
* God attends the funerals of sparrows
* Those who can't ring the bell often knock
* Suppose like ball players our errors were published daily!
* Don't say, "Our Father" on Sunday, then rest of week act like orphan
* You can be so smart you're totally miserable!
* Small leaks can sink a ship!
* Squeaking wheels get grease, but often replacement!
* You can take it with you by sending it ahead
* A horse doesn't kick while he's pulling
* Your soul is the world's greatest battlefield
* Careful: Your thoughts may break into words anytime!
* Faultfinders are not usually from the ranks of the faultless

* Kids get spoiled because it's hard to spank grandmothers!
* At the end of your rope? Tie a knot and hang on!
* A constant liar needs a very good memory
* In covering the subject, don't smother it!
* You get good judgment from using bad judgment
* People will believe anything if you whisper it!
* Sure money talks! It says, "Good-bye!"
* With two eyes, one tongue, we're to see twice what we say!
* Credit is a system of buying on the lay-awake plan!
* Don't laugh in a person's face behind his back!
* Like boats, people make loud noises when in a fog!
* Like checks, don't endorse rumors unless genuine!
* Societies honor life conformists and dead troublemakers!
* If you must cry over spilt milk, condense it!
* Remember: This earth is also disposable!
* "Nothing needs reforming more than other's habits." — Twain
* Do you look down on people who look down on people?
* You know your rights but do you know your wrongs?
* God's best soldiers come from the highlands of affliction
* "There are no gains without pains!" — Franklin
* Resistance to disease depends on the quality of living
* Today put on something warm — S M I L E !
* Wrecking neighbor's house doesn't improve yours!
* "Anger" is one letter short of "danger"!
* Harder to keep than money is quiet!
* A battery has life only when it is charged
* Guns don't kill people — people kill people!
* Failure is the path of least persistence!
* Laugh about something every day, even if it is only yourself!
* "Don't expect all blue skies!" — African saying
* Great discoveries often come when a trifle stubs its toe!
* Tears of self-pity block out God!
* One today is worth a dozen tomorrows!
* "Never trouble trouble 'til trouble troubles you!"
* Better wish you'd said it than you hadn't!
* No great poem has been written in a crowd!
* Pretending riches keeps a lot of people poor!

* All people smile in the same language!
* The best gifts are tied with heartstrings!
* Hurried life is empty life!
* To the critical the whole world is at fault!
* Of two evils choose neither!
* As with a motor, something's wrong when we knock!
* Listen to them and they will listen to you!
* Do you ever bleed from "spur of the moment"?
* Little pots are soon hot!
* As with money, the more knowledge you have, the less you brag!
* "I'll mend my ways, God — but not today."
* Today is the tomorrow you worried about yesterday
* Those who need advice most like it least
* Gossip is like an egg — once hatched, it has wings!
* Thinking is when the mouth stops, head talks to itself!
* Better be square than move in the wrong circles!
* A fling often carries a sting!
* In driving and baseball it's getting home safely that counts!
* No man ever became a genius by just claiming to be one!
* What on earth are you doing, for heaven's sake?
* Learn to cooperate with the inevitable!
* Good boss — one who gets three men to do three men's work!
* Some things are even worth doing badly!
* The road to success is usually under construction
* The unmapped country is largely within us
* "The reward of a thing well done is to have done it." — Emerson
* For empty living, pick good excuses, stay with them!
* Being cool is not now cool — not being cool is cool!
* Mind-expanding trips available at our local library
* Gossip — ear pollution
* Wisdom comes from biting off more than you can chew
* It's better to light a candle than to curse the darkness
* Doctor with stethoscope to patient: "All I get is the busy signal!"
* The first Adam-splitting brought forth Eve!
* A good scare is worth more than good advice!
* If yesterday's deeds look big, you haven't done much today!

* A doctor never scolds a physical ailment
* A clique is a friendship group gone to seed
* If God seems far away, who moved?
* "One swallow doesn't bring a summer" but many bring a fall!
* Yesterday is a rearview mirror!
* Changed men change society
* Gossip goes faster over the sour grapevine
* The knocker is always outside the door!
* Can you spot hypocrites? Takes one to know one!
* The wildest colts sometimes make the best horses
* Little boy: "Mommy, are we alive or on tape?"
* Digging for facts is better than jumping to conclusions
* It's also blessed to receive!
* Beware of the barrenness of busyness
* Nothing improves the vision more than hindsight!
* When all is said and done, usually more is said than done!
* Easy come, easy go!
* Of all the arts, the most backward is thinking
* Replace your bad habits with good ones!
* Opportunity wears soft-soled shoes
* Nothing is more soluble in alcohol than conscience!
* People don't care what happens if it's not to them!
* The human race has improved on everything except people
* Come to church early and get a back seat!
* Why some don't mind own business: 1. no mind; 2. no business
* It's what you learn after you know it all that counts
* "Home permanent" a mother with small children
* Great movements were born of human need
* Sympathy is two hearts at one load
* What about taking the advice you give others?
* The drunk was driving because "I'm in no condition to walk!"
* When you stop to think, don't stay parked!
* Muddy the stream of life and you'll drink dirty water!
* Announcement: Utopia is still in the talking stage
* When God calls, turn up your hearing aid!
* Drive as if a police car is always ahead of you!
* A person talking about his inferiors hasn't any

* Early to rise, early to bed — makes us healthy and socially dead
* Janitor: "I've seen 12 preachers come and go, still believe in God!"
* The old rugged cross looks good "on a hill and far away"
* Lie about others as you would like them to lie about you!
* Before letting self go, be sure you can get it back!
* You're young only once — after that you need another excuse!
* Gossip: "I must stop — I've told more than I heard, already!"
* Sometimes you need to take bull by tail, look the situation in face!
* It's hard to make footprints on time's sands, sitting down!
* Nobody don't never git nothin' for nothin' no where, no how!
* Some see the handwriting on the wall — they just can't read it!
* Absence makes the heart go wander!
* "God, give me patience — right now!"
* Cancer cures smoking!
* For that run-down feeling, try jaywalking!
* Harder than breaking a habit — not telling how you did it!
* "All things come of thee, O Lord — and of thine own have we given thee 10¢!"
* Blowing your stack adds to pollution
* "He's often wrong, but never in doubt!"
* There are some things that every girl should "no"
* A man in love with dimples shouldn't marry the whole girl!
* Do not put off until tomorrow what you shouldn't do today
* Closing mouth keeps ignorance from leaking out!
* Golf is to yell, "Fore," take six, put down five!
* Drunk: To feel sophisticated, not be able to pronounce it!
* Nothing adds heat to arguments like rubbing two car fenders together
* You fall on your face faster when you hit the ceiling!
* Why didn't Noah just swat both flies?
* Why did Moses take cheese into the ark?
* Overeating makes you think at your stomach!
* Alcohol kills the living and preserves the dead

* Little boy: "Bring up a child and away he goes!"
* Quit fighting battles you've already won!
* Pessimists see through morose-colored glasses!
* To win an argument is to lose a friend
* Candles exhaust themselves in giving light
* Most fat comes from eating too much!
* What good is 11th hour conversation if you die at 10:30?
* Drive slow! Our squirrels don't know one nut from another!
* Boy: "The twins in the Bible were I and II Samuel!"
* "Who washed the dishes at the Last Supper?"
* Tears of self-pity block out God!
* To get your head above the crowd you must stick it out!
* The real name for voluntary inertia is laziness!
* Destiny shapes ends, middles are of our own chewsing!
* Ideal wife — woman with ideal husband!
* When brushing teeth don't bother to sharpen tongue!
* To take it with you, send it ahead!
* Girls — a ring on the hand is worth two in the voice!
* To his senses man needs to add two: horse and common!
* Who wants to hear how they did it when you were young?
* Nothing is "opened by mistake" more than the mouth!
* Guilt: Truth ache!
* Class reunion — a get-together to see who's falling apart!
* A place in the sun calls for a few blisters!
* You can smoke and go to heaven — even ahead of time!
* Old taxes never die — they just change their names
* Science class ... playing fool ... bang! bang! ... no school!
* Three ages of man: Youth, middle, and "you're looking well!"
* "I may have my faults but one is not being wrong!"
* Do you ever get your tang all tongueled up?
* Patience — ability to count down when you want to blast off!
* He who slings mud loses ground!
* The wrong way to pick friends is to pieces!
* Pollution is a dirty shame!
* Looking down your nose you get the wrong slant!
* Looking for the needy? Try the mirror!
* The first lie detector was made from Adam's rib!

* Children not only comfort old age, they help reach it faster!
* How do you think of God when a cow steps on your foot?
* When your cup runneth over, slosh some on somebody!
* Even a bad life can be used as a bad example!
* Remember: The day has to face you, too!
* The more you sit the less you can stand!
* If in doubt, don't do it!
* Every word you speak makes a circle and returns to you
* Life at its best is always disciplined
* Experience you get when you're looking for something else
* Your ship won't come in unless you've sent one out
* The oak is an acorn that held its ground!
* Fences should be low enough to permit handshaking
* To sleep, count sheep or better, talk with the shepherd!
* A switch in time saves crime! — Newell
* It's easier to float rumors than to sink them!
* When swallowing your own medicine the spoon seems large!
* "I can live for two months on a good compliment!" — Twain
* Unless you stand for something you fall for anything
* Like black coffee, good communication is hard to sleep after!
* Opportunist — one who does what you intended to do!
* Some churchmen are "seventh day absentists"
* Girl: "Always be sincere, whether you mean it or not!"
* The water that doesn't fill the jar makes most noise
* Shoe shop sign: "We mend soles and gladly dye for you."
* You know how a skunk solves his problems!
* "I believe 100% in half of what you say."
* It's hard to sink half a ship!
* Don't keep the faith, baby — share it!
* Best thing to do behind his back — pat it!
* To be happy ever after, don't be after too much!
* Middle age: When all you exercise is caution
* The man who never made a mistake has a wife who did!
* Wise Solomon had so many wives to advise him!
* Some believe they're as good as they never were!
* Prejudice: A disease from hardening of the categories!
* We older ones can tell it like it was!

* Little boy: "The fight started when he hit me back!"
* Don't trip over the weekend!
* To make ends meet, get off your own!
* Wisdom: Don't use your influence till you have it!
* Middle age: When you don't have to have fun to enjoy yourself!
* Ulcers come from mountain climbing over molehills!
* Future: When you wish you'd done what you're not doing now!
* The rich get richer, poor get credit cards!
* Watch half-truths — you might get the wrong half!
* Wanted: An alarm clock to help us rise to the occasion!
* Pessimist: Burns bridges before he gets to them!
* The closed mouth gathers no foot!
* What you don't eat won't go to waist!
* To drive a baby buggy — tickle his feet!
* If you're not a sinner, bring one who is!
* "He doesn't lie — he just remembers big!"
* Ivory hunter's problem: There's an elephant attached!
* Many fishermen catch fish by the tale
* Reckless drivers are drivers of extinction
* No fool's like an old fool — you can't beat experience!
* A pessimist is one who lives with an optimist
* Dieters, remember: "Taste makes waste!"
* "They say most geniuses are conceited. I'm not!"
* Pollution: Sootprints!
* Chips on the shoulder seem to come from the head!
* Put off to tomorrow what you'll botch today!
* The straightest man in the Bible? Joseph. He became a ruler.
* Would a psychiatrist want a cuckoo clock?
* Roses red, violets blue, orchids $10, would dandelions do?
* Worry is as useless as whispering in a boiler factory!
* It's not bad to be a nut if you're on the right bolt!
* It wasn't raining when Noah built the ark!
* To break a bad habit — drop it!

QUOTES ABOUT GOD

* Man is meant to glorify God!
* Isn't it time to stop playing God?
* God is God of our inner storms!
* Today: Let God fill your mind
* God's peace surpasses our fondest dreams!
* God is more ready to forgive than we are to receive!
* In God's love you have super-joy!
* God, help me to change what can be changed!
* God, give me the serenity to accept what can't be changed!
* God, give me wisdom to know what can and can't be changed!
* For real abundant life say a big "Yes," to God!
* God knows your need before you do!
* Today practice unlimiting God!
* When God shuts one door, he opens another!
* There never was a time when God didn't exist!
* Blessed are the peacemakers — sons of God!
* "The dawn is God shouting for joy" — Blake
* God so loved the world he didn't send a committee!
* God's love never runs out!
* Trivialities block God!
* Tell God of the gratitude in your heart
* God is my ultimate security
* A pure heart is single-minded toward God!
* "Putting God first" is not to protect him!
* Those in harmony with God go forward even in sleep!
* You can discuss him all your life without facing God!
* "Be still and know that I am God." — Psalm 46:10
* Sickness is the way God sometimes gets into a life
* Cast your burden upon the Lord and he shall help you!
* Lonely? God is a never-failing companion
* Are you in God's way, or in the "way of God"?
* God's voice is gentle — don't ignore it!
* Just being there for God can be valuable!
* God is greater than any of our problems
* God's peace laughs in the face of death

* God is not an absentee land owner!
* "Lord, use my service, if only in an advisory capacity!"
* God puts his moral law into our hearts!
* "God hides things by putting them near us." — Emerson
* Man wants God, but in his own way!
* In all, God works for good with those who love him!
* Man's biggest ideas are from God!
* God gives men supernatural courage
* God measures by your heart, not your head!
* God can repair your torn up self
* Obey God's laws willingly or learn unwillingly
* Be willing today to be used by God!
* With God we must be poor enough to receive
* God's love is not conditional
* God weighs man's intentions as well as his deeds
* Man tries to kill God and become a God himself
* We accept a God who is fair but not one who forgives!
* God is always being power!
* God is a very present help in trouble
* We enter God's kingdom by losing "respectable goodness"
* God does not give his gifts accidentally
* You don't drift into the kingdom of God!
* If we ask God and listen, we will not fail!
* What on earth has God to do with peace?
* All we are saying is "Give God a chance"
* God wants to knock pretence and pious pose out of us
* God never operates human museums
* God sows his saints by his whirlwind
* God continually introduces us to some we don't like!
* God is slowly wearing the pyramids away!
* God loves us in spite of our foolishness
* God made us, not we ourselves!
* Give thanks to the Lord, for he is good!
* The heart, not sure of God, fears to laugh in his presence
* Whatever the heart relies on is its God
* In God we grow
* "God pounds our soft spots to toughen us up!" — Paul White

* We hear God best when self is silent
* If creation should vanish, God would still be God!
* We are made by God for his glory
* Are you where God wants you now?
* God's resources are never exhausted!
* God changes our hearts — we must change our minds
* God needs more mature people in right places
* God has already done it — forgive yourself!
* God can't heal if you won't be made whole!
* Amazing! God treats us as if we're righteous!
* If God accepts you, why can't you accept yourself?
* Are you God's enemy?
* God promises no bed of roses
* No life is too broken for God to repair
* The great fact of life: God is available!
* "Lost" means living as if there's no God who cares!
* Obey God, and leave the consequences to him!
* God's peace is from springs too deep for life's droughts
* "Once you were no people — now you are God's people!"
* It takes time for God to reveal himself!
* Live cheerfully, think hopefully — God is here!
* No "snow job" ever fooled God!
* Magic, black or white, is a wrong substitute for following God
* Character is what God knows you are!
* He's still got the whole world in his hands!
* God's place can bring costly conflict
* God's answers are wiser than our prayers
* God's blessings look so much like something you earned!
* Wait patiently for God — rest in him!
* God shows himself to those who really want him!
* Does God grade on the curve?
* God does things to us and through us
* God's truth frees but often hurts
* God is composer — Christians are his notes
* God's yoke — when he puts his arms around our necks
* God may come in a burning issue, not a burning bush
* God won't lead you where he won't illuminate you!

* Some would give up lives for God but not reputations!
* No human need or pain is beyond God's concern
* "God loves you and I'm trying"
* God is about God's business — are you?
* God is against what is destructive for people
* God, make me ashamed of my vain self-centeredness!

QUOTES ABOUT JESUS

* Jesus is "the real thing"!
* Jesus wanted more to be good than to "have it good"
* If you're empty enough, Jesus can fill you with peace
* Jesus can make you clean, pure, holy!
* "Jesus, I didn't know I was hungry until I met you"
* "I will never leave you nor forsake you." — Jesus
* "Jesus is chiseling his love on my heart." — Teenager
* When Jesus called Peter "Rock" he gave him strength
* No man could ever invent a person like Jesus!
* Nobody but Jesus can really make you whole
* Jesus was not ashamed to be with the unacceptable
* "Formalism in religion crucified Christ." — Tournier
* The size of the tool doesn't matter in the Master's hand
* Jesus is God's "personal illustration"
* Jesus is absolutely decisive for every man
* This is the Jesus generation
* Christ doesn't promise exemption from trouble
* "Come to me all who are weary and I will give you rest!"
* Jesus is the planned focus of God in human history
* Jesus is the way, the truth, the life
* Jesus is God's word become flesh
* Jesus never preached scarcity
* When the crowd got big Jesus said, "Deny self," and half departed
* Jesus Christ is a "different drummer"
* You can do all things through Christ, who strengthens you!
* "Christ in us" seems too good to be true!
* There is no situation that Jesus cannot master
* Jesus invented nothing new — he was new!
* Jesus is our contemporary fixed point!
* Christ is the "eternal trip"
* Jesus died that you might live — think of that!
* Jesus saves us not from circumstance but from ourselves
* Jesus makes man at one with his highest self
* "Greater works than I do shall ye do!" — Jesus

* Jesus will not save the world alone!
* In Jesus, old things pass away, all becomes new!
* Turning on to Jesus is the best "trip"
* Christ lives in the man whose life is open to him
* Jesus calls you to awake to your hidden depths
* Have you deliberately committed your will to Jesus Christ?
* When Jesus said, "Take up a cross," most of his cross melted away!
* "You want to argue? I can't. I choose Christ!" — G. A. Kennedy
* Jesus said those not for him are against him
* Jesus Christ wants you!
* You can talk for years and not come face to face with Christ
* Christ can change your self-hate
* From Jesus is that spiritual power that makes you whole
* "I came that you have life!" — Jesus
* "I will never leave you nor forsake you!" — Jesus
* Christ helps us not to avoid suffering but to overcome it
* Jesus didn't lose his life — he gave it
* Joy comes from Jesus first, others, then yourself
* Jesus lost no dignity getting on his knees
* Jesus is God's face!
* Jesus gets you tuned in, turned on, and toned up!
* A brother would die for a brother, right? Jesus did just that!
* Jesus Christ brought God's good revolution
* Bet your life on Jesus!
* Want to change the world? So does Jesus!
* Lost? Confused? Things not going right? Jesus has the answers
* You can't "go back to Christ" — he's up ahead!
* Trying to find yourself? Talk it over with Jesus
* If you just be like other men, don't accept Jesus Christ
* When was the last time you really looked at Jesus?
* When Buddha died, he had to go to Jesus!
* Jesus "knows what is in man" but still loves us! Great!
* He who lives without Christ is a spiritual bankrupt
* "Be of good cheer, I have overcome the world!" — Jesus
* "Lose your life for my sake and find it!" — Jesus
* Jesus is the real bridge between things and persons

* When we know who Jesus is, we know who we are!
* Jesus never taught quiet, private religion
* Jesus never defended himself!
* The heart is an organ — Let the Master tune it!
* Are you and Jesus going in the same direction?
* Jesus can make you a new person — We'll tell you how
* Deny yourself, take your cross, follow Jesus
* "He who shall lose his life for my sake shall find it!"
* Jesus didn't promise ecstasy so much as a cross
* Jesus, not man, is the real image of God!
* Christ is still "the great disturber"
* Bet your life that Christ is right!
* Jesus is either an imposter or his claims are true!
* "I am with you always." — Jesus
* Jesus is "God approachable"!
* Why don't you just ask Jesus into your heart now?
* Jesus practiced everything he preached
* Jesus took a weak chain of men and made it strong
* Only Jesus can cure soul-sickness
* Jesus understands you!
* Accepting Christ — simple, yes; easy, no
* Jesus is so great he can afford to be gentle
* Treachery built a cross — indifference keeps Christ on it
* "Love one another as I have loved you." — Jesus
* Jesus is our bridge over troubled water
* Jesus promises treasure in heaven, a cross here!
* Christ can restore your collapsed personality
* Jesus is equal to all the needs you may have
* Some follow Jesus with enthusiasm until cross time
* Under Christ, death is no more "ultimate disaster"
* Jesus brings the good news: "The judge forgives!"
* Jesus is the decisive man for every man
* Accredited spokesmen called Jesus a fraud!
* Jesus transforms "believers" into brothers
* With Christ religiosity chokes in our throats!
* Jesus not only solves problems, he dissolves them!
* What about playing your whole life to a living Jesus?

* The Holy Spirit gives ordinary men extraordinary power!
* Joy is the window cleaner of the Spirit
* The sin against the Holy Spirit is to say, "No," to God
* The Holy Spirit gives power to disagree without being disagreeable
* The Holy Spirit is sometimes the dis-comforter!
* The church does not control the Holy Spirit
* Fruits of the Spirit: love, joy, peace, faith, gentleness
* You can never go where God is not
* You're not a nobody — you're a child of God!
* If you make your bed in hell, God is there!
* You and God could make a great team!
* When a child asks, "Who made God?" what would you say?
* God can give you the courage you need
* God and you can handle all your problems
* Are you serving the Lord with gladness?
* You are important because God loves you!
* Did you know that God is a "spiritual garbage collector"?
* You are important to God in his scheme of things
* God won't look for your medals or diplomas, but scars
* When you say, "God, I'm in trouble," he listens

FAITH, HOPE, LOVE

* Faith is giving God the problems you can't handle
* Faith never looks at appearances
* You swim by trusting the water
* "I ask not for faith to move mountains, just to move me!"
* While there's life there's hope!
* "The beginning of true faith is the end of anxiety." — George Mueller
* Not many are drawn into faith by arguments!
* To get faith: Admit you want it, then go where it is!
* Faith is to know that God is with you!
* Faith is becoming aware of God and our immortality
* Faith is the substance of things hoped for, the evidence of things unseen
* Things are never so bad that one should have no hope!
* "Faith must not evaporate in the hand!" — Keck
* Your great act of faith is to decide you're not God!
* Faith is a fire in the heart
* Faith doesn't know where it's being led but knows who's leading
* Secularism is a faith
* Faith must become something or it becomes nothing
* True faith doesn't try to dictate to God
* We walk by faith, not by sight
* Faith says, "It will not always be this way!"
* Our faith in God is our security
* God works through those who have faith, patience, determination
* Faith is a borrower who brings a blank check
* Faith is "A prayer-for-rain" who takes an umbrella!
* We need to relate personal faith to the world situation
* Do you need more faith in faith?
* "Lord, I have about enough faith for one grain ..."
* Faith and doubt can co-exist!
* Where there's no faith in future there's no power in present!
* Faith is giving God your anxiety and guilt!

* The cost of real faith is to give up secondary security
* All things are possible to him who believes!
* "One certainty we have — love is permanent!" — Ray Veh
* We need love, especially when we don't deserve it!
* Selfishness breaks the law of love!
* Love or perish!
* The law of love is the law of the universe
* "Love one another as I have loved you." — Jesus
* "No one has greater love than to lay down his life for a friend"
* Today: Reach out with love!
* Love is deeply caring!
* Love enriches the life of giver and receiver — everybody wins!
* With his loving spirit in us, we deal with each other as God does!
* Love will dig into the gutter to find and lift people
* Love looks forward — hate looks back!
* With love we can disagree without being disagreeable!
* Love is pouring out affection on retarded children
* Love can win where force and violence fails
* People don't need our advice as much as our love
* Perfect love casts out fear!
* God wrapped his love in a person!
* You may wander far, but God's love has a long arm
* Today — tell somebody you love that you love them!
* God is always being love!
* When love is present, you can do a lot!
* Love is a blessed boomerang!
* Love the human mind can't understand — only accept
* Love cannot be wasted!
* Despair hurts love, but love can overcome despair
* Love releases imprisoned splendor in people
* Respect and love, like charity, begin at home
* "Lord, help me today to want to love people for you"
* Perfect love overcomes fear
* The attitude of love is gratitude
* The love of money is the root of much evil
* All wars begin before the first shot is fired
* Say your love with gestures and praise

LOVE

* Our deep need is for someone to love
* Of faith, hope, and love, the greatest is love!
* Love hardly notices when others do it wrong!
* We're to love God with heart and soul before mind and strength!
* True charity is loving those who do not love you
* Real love "moves from the tutti-frutti to the nitty-gritty"
* The law of love is greater than the law of "law"
* Today: Speak the language of love
* We love others from the bedrock of God's love for us!
* Love bears all things — believes, hopes all things!
* Real love feels the hurt of others and wants to heal it!
* Love doesn't happen by chance
* Drugs can't overcome disillusionment, but love can!
* 4-letter words to explain sex: Help, give, care, love!
* Love never gives up!
* Love is eternal!
* Love is patient!
* God is love!
* The cross is the meeting place of love with sin
* God is always being love
* Love one another!
* Give love and get love!
* "I bet my life on beauty, truth, and love!"
* Love is quicksand — clutch it and it goes away!
* Love is infinitely patient
* With love, the more you give away the more you have!
* Love is not stuck up nor "up tight" — Johnny Robinson
* Love never cops out!
* Learn the law of love and live it!
* Pure religion is love in action!
* Love is God's greatest weapon!
* Faith, hope, and love aren't as good in half-sizes!
* Love is an active verb!
* Love on your own terms is not love at all!

* "Where love is there God is!" — Tolstoy
* "God so loved the world that he gave ..."
* Love is the deepest need of our time!
* Cultivate the ability to love living!
* God loves the unlovely!
* To walk away from hate, walk toward love
* God sends us not so much to preach as to love
* Jesus did not try to be a "lovable person"
* We love God because he first loved us
* Stupendous! God's amazing love for man!
* Hurt people, hurt people, but love heals
* Think of how deep is your need for love
* Love is giving a lift when the going is tough
* As we give love we learn to receive God's love
* God is the world's greatest lover!
* Love never fails!
* Calvary was the world's greatest love-in!
* Christian love means the helping hand
* Love your neighbor — it's too crowded to hate him!
* Love is the salt of life
* God loves you, no matter who you are!
* God's love is broader than man's mind
* A God of love made moral law — we pay when we break it!
* Do what love demands — for Christ's sake!
* Those who condemn usually have little love
* Love your enemies and let them tell your faults
* Love cures more than condemnation
* Love and leave the future to God
* Really loving God is giving up self
* "Born again" gives a new capacity to love
* We are to love the unlovable!
* If love is blind, fear is more so!

CHRISTIAN SERVICE

* When God says, "Do it," do it!
* Better teach to fish than give a fish!
* God never planned that we only do nice things for him
* If yesterday's deeds look big, you haven't done much today!
* "Our vocation is to serve other people!" — Tolstoy
* Today try binding the wounds on other's souls!
* The smallest deed is better than the grandest intention
* God values not so much "ability" as "usability"
* Self-centered service does not draw us closer to God!
* What about helping God get into the worst places?
* The woods would be silent if only the best birds sang!
* To dream about it when you should be doing it is wrong!
* God measures loyalty by unselfish service to those in need
* Help God give the hungry food, the thirsty, drink!
* Sign over sink: "Divine services here three times daily!"
* He who gives much is richest!
* Good done to the least is done to God!
* "The doing of little things makes a great life!" — Eugenia Price
* What has God to do with what you're doing?
* Service to God grows from what we are!
* "He who shall lose his life for my sake shall find it."
* Been to jail lately?
* Service is the rent we pay for room on earth!
* "Meek" means moldability, God-controlled
* God does not want "live and let live" indifference!
* The test for saints is not preaching but washing feet!
* When church service is over, our service begins!
* Attempt great things for God!
* Little comes from only talking about it!
* Charity gives itself rich: stinginess hoards itself poor!
* Work is love made visible!
* Trust God with tomorrow — help somebody today!
* Today: Somebody lonely needs you!
* What you do for others will live beyond you!
* Service to God grows from what we are!

* Look what Jesus did with a towel!
* God needs you to turn someone's boredom to joy!
* To live is to serve — to serve is to share
* Live and help live!
* When you are God's you can't say where he will put you!
* Our business is to do what lies clearly at hand!
* Look around you ... select a need and put love to work!
* "The reward of a thing well done is to have done it." — Emerson
* Do it now and you'll have time for something else!
* God needs you to help bring a life from despair!
* Full service demands a full heart!
* People doubt what you say, believe what you do!
* To lighten life's load, lift the weight from someone's back!
* We can learn to do most things that Jesus did!
* The vocation of every Christian is to serve others
* Are you looking for a "way out" or a way for God to use you?
* It's wrong to live only by ideas — use your hands and feet!
* In God's service is perfect freedom!
* For full life say to God, "Here am I. Send me!"
* Be not simply good, but good for something!
* Unless God checks, work where abilities meet the world's needs

HEALING

* God will heal you now!
* "When the heart is sick, we're sick all over." — Mann
* A doctor doesn't heal by touching up x-rays
* "Earth has no sorrow that heaven cannot heal"
* Today — try binding the wounds on people's souls!
* Men are often sick for not living in God's purpose
* Our bodies are made for good will
* Jesus keeps you from being spiritually bedridden
* Sickness may come from unwise living
* There's powerful healing in creative silence
* Sickness of soul is often passed on to our bodies
* Enjoying ill health?

SIN, SALVATION

* Salvation is to be saved from self
* Repentance is not "regret" but turning around
* God doesn't fight sin by avoiding sinners
* Modern man needs to admit the reality of evil
* "Phony" is another name for sinner
* Overcome evil with good!
* God can give you "a new set of spiritual eyes"
* In being "born again" there are sometimes deformities!
* Sin looks God in the face and says, "I won't!"
* The wages of sin is death
* "Let whoever never sinned cast the first stone!"
* All sinners are by choice
* The prodigal son said the healing words, "I have sinned"
* Anything that keeps you from being the person God wants is sin
* Love of money is the root of all evil
* "Our greatest fault — being conscious of others' faults" — Gibran
* We have been free to choose evil since Eden!
* The center of sin is making ourselves God!
* Sin is separation but Jesus is our bridge
* The wages of sin are not frozen
* Whatever a person sows, he reaps!
* Long regret is high price for short pleasure!
* The cross is the place where love and sin meet
* We all sit down to a banquet of consequences
* God changes short-term evil to long-term good!
* The greatest sinner is often not aware of it!
* We can sin by silence!
* The sinful self has to look away from death
* Your sins don't shock God — talk them over!
* Panic in the presence of evil is pagan
* "The sins of my times are partly my own!"
* God's name for sin is "sin"
* Sin is often more against ourselves than God

* Sin is anything God doesn't want in our lives
* True confession is as painful as any other surgery!
* Confusing others' defects won't solve your problem!
* Remorse is not necessarily full repentance!
* If we confess, God will forgive us and cleanse us
* What if God waited until we were adequate?
* To God surrender not only your vices but yourself
* "You have sinned, and come short of the glory of God!"
* Evil is real, and must be fought to be defeated
* God sends salvation free but doesn't pay postage
* It's not too late to repent!
* God cannot make us sons without our consent
* God's invitation: "Come." His command, "Go."
* God doesn't slow you down — he changes your direction
* Jesus doesn't call us to judge but to confess
* Stop rebelling against God
* God condemns evil by letting it work itself out
* "Seek first the kingdom and God's righteousness"
* It's one thing to praise discipline, another to submit
* Sin makes you a slave — Jesus frees you!
* The great warfare is between God and us who rebel

CHRISTIAN

* "Christian" means living the gospel at your address
* "Christians" are ready to change things if they can be done nicely
* Real Christians have been invaded by the spirit of God
* If you were arrested as "Christian" would evidence convict you?
* God is composer; Christians, his notes!
* Being a Christian can mean getting into trouble
* Christians view life with the thousand year look
* A Christian can be as materialistic as any communist!
* "Church member" doesn't automatically mean you're Christian!
* A Christian knows "joy in tribulation"
* Great Christians doubt, but don't stay that way!
* True Christians are ready to wash feet
* Christianity is not a theory — it is a life!
* Are you AWOL from Christian responsibility?
* Can you imagine a "Christian" pessimist?
* The real Christian couldn't care more!
* How would the gospel grow if only you spread it!
* What have you done today that only a Christian would do?
* Can a Christian ever "retire"?
* When you're fed up with yourself, God can change you!
* The world's great need — people who know God personally
* "Real Christian" — one who could give his parrot to a gossip
* A Christian without a church is like a bee without a hive!
* Do you have a full freezer but lack spiritual food?
* Are you a light for God who flickered out?
* The Christian allows God to "do his thing" through him!
* Christians have a higher law — love!
* A Christian is one who knows he's being forgiven!
* Christians belong to God's construction crew!
* The Christian says, "Whatever it takes ..."
* Little sins don't stay little
* Christians are to protect the innocent from hurt

* Sin: Wanting your own way more than God's way
* Are you too busy acting like a Christian to be one?
* Unbelievers have no monopoly on intelligence
* A "moderately good Christian" is like a "moderately good egg"
* "They'll know we are Christians by our love"
* For the best fire, put together several logs!
* Through you today will anybody know "God so loved..."?
* The outward characteristic of a Christian is joy
* Can there be such a thing as a selfish Christian?
* The gospel — one beggar telling another where to find bread
* True Christianity is rooted in both God and man
* "My father is a Christian but not practicing at present"
* "Christian" can't mean intolerant, jealous, suspicious!
* A little Christian habit can be a false God
* Religion divorced from life is not Christ-like religion

BIBLE

* If you couldn't get another, what's your Bible worth?
* The gospel is an anvil wearing out many hammers
* Have you read the "good book" lately?
* Matthew 5-7 gives you instructions!
* Boil down psychology and you get the Sermon on the Mount!
* The New Testament speaks with new certainty — check it!
* The gospel is not "good views" but good news!
* The Bible is not first of moral standards but of God's love
* Christ's resurrection is mentioned 108 times in the New Testament
* "Praise" and "rejoice" are in the Bible 550 times!
* The book of Matthew uses the word "immediately" 17 times!
* "The Bible throws light on the commentaries."
* The Beatitudes are eight paths to God (Matthew 5)
* New Bible translations are like cleaned fine old pictures!
* Let the New Testament be your guide until something better comes
* In the Bible David fell in an idle moment
* If you lack faith, really examine the New Testament!
* The New Testament views resurrection with deep certainty

DEALING WITH THE NEGATIVES
(Satan, Enemies, Guilt, Trouble, Worry, Hate, Fear, Suffering)

* Resist Satan and he will flee from you!
* The devil can only suggest!
* When one finds the truth, Satan helps him organize it!
* The devil's chief trick is proving there is none!
* The devil loves generalities and postponed action!
* After all, the devil succeeds too!
* Satan takes out bitterness on man through man
* Satan doesn't fight those going in his same direction
* Satan leaves you alone when you stay away from God!
* Satan's great word is "wait"
* "The devil hath power to assume a pleasing shape!" — Hamlet
* How will "evil ones" ever know of the love of God?
* To give evil for evil is cleaning off dirt with mud!
* The devil likes to say, "There's plenty of time!"
* Love your enemies — confuse them!
* Our enemies are largely within us
* Don't make enemies — friends are hard enough on you!
* The kingdom is to be in the midst of your enemies!
* Speak well of your enemies — you made them!
* Negativism breeds negativism!
* Repentance is being sorry for what you've quit doing
* "The wise learn only from their own guilt!" — Jung
* Guilt is usually suspicious!
* Guilt is fear of being found out and punished
* We suffer when we know we're dishonest
* Our guilt must either be forgiven or punished
* When you hear "guilt" what comes to your mind?
* "Only a fool is interested in others' guilt!" — Jung
* God hides growth in big, tough problems
* Are you a genius at expecting trouble?
* "Honesty" can be brutal
* Smart people don't solve problems part way
* Save yourself trouble by not borrowing any
* Trouble is opportunity in work clothes

* Every problem has a soft spot
* "Present sufferings are nothing to the glory to come!"
* With a well-trained memory you forget yesterday's troubles
* "Stress is the root cause of all disease" — Dr. Hans Seelye
* Focus on problems and you become problem-centered
* Never trouble trouble 'til trouble troubles you!
* Trouble doesn't interrupt life — it is life!
* Like babies, troubles grow from nursing
* Anxiety has eyes all over its head
* "Worry is a stream of fear, cutting a gorge through us"
* The cross of restless anxiety is not from God!
* You're not pitiful, either!
* Worry is today's mouse eating tomorrow's cheese
* Worry is contagious!
* To take the path of worry is to let go of God's hand
* Worry divides the mind
* Worry is public enemy no. 1
* Walk your worries away
* Don't brood over the past — now is too important!
* "Don't worry over life's necessities and miss its purpose!"

PRAYER

* Prayer is a spiritual bath in the love of God
* God's answers are wiser than our prayers
* Prayer is the eye of the soul
* Daily prayers lessen daily cares!
* "Pray devoutly, hammer stoutly!" — English proverb
* Prayer is conscious communication with the infinite spirit
* Feel like a "piece of nothing"? Come in and pray!
* Praying is also "waiting on the Lord"!
* Through prayer you can be reunited with your source!
* Prayer is giving self to God and taking what he offers
* God wants us to take everything to him!
* "On your knees, you are taller than trees!"
* "Thy will be done on earth" is a call to action!
* Prayer really can change your life!
* Pray for God's will in small things!
* Prayer is tuning in!
* All prayer is answered, "yes," "no," or "wait"!
* Prayer is oil for the daily grind!
* You're not praying to a static God!
* God is able to do more than we think or ask!
* Prayer increases our faith and self-knowledge!
* Prayer produces peace and calm
* Rufus mostly said: "Prayer unmesses the messer!"
* You're welcome at our altar right now!
* When there's no way out, there's a way up!
* Give your closet skeletons a decent burial at our altar!
* Prayer — the key of the day, the security of the night!
* Pray freely — God is not shocked by our sins!
* All things are possible to him who believes!
* "God, help me to accept those unlike me!"
* Prayer brings illumination
* 6-year-old after prayer: "God took the madness out of me!"
* To get on your feet, get on your knees!
* "Create in me a clean heart, O God!"
* Great praying starts with great believing

* "Lord, when I'm wrong, make me willing to change!"
* Sing, as well as pray, without ceasing!
* This church offers prayer for healing to anyone
* "Lord, make me an instrument of your peace!"
* "Lord, forgive our short tempers and longer ones, too!"
* No activity is more important than a quiet time
* Prayer increases ability to face life creatively
* Some who pray for eternal life can't fill rainy afternoons!
* Real prayer relaxes body, mind, soul
* To strengthen faith, recall answered prayers
* "O taste and see that the Lord is good!"
* Today reserve a half-hour for meditation
* In prayer, offer God your spiritual garbage
* Pray for some enemy right now!
* Man's greatest power is the power of prayer
* "Cry to the Lord in your trouble — he will deliver you"
* Daily devotions clear mixed emotions!
* Today: Tell God exactly how you feel!
* Watch for God in the events that follow prayer
* Prayer is the most perfect form of energy!
* Real prayer seeks God's will, not our own
* Work while you pray and pray while you work!
* "Have mercy, O God — blot out my transgressions!"
* Prayer is constant communion with God!
* Let go and let God!
* "Forgive me, Lord, for trying to tell you what to do!"
* "Thy will be done" is a prayer for change
* You don't have to talk with God in Old English!
* Prayer is the only power to overcome the "laws of nature"
* "Forgive us, Lord, for viewing the world with dry eyes!"
* As with our bodies, prayer life develops with exercise!
* Negative thoughts can block out God's prayer answers
* Hello! Try our altar for size — it's open!

QUOTES ABOUT "YOU"

* Let the peace of God rule your heart
* "Tell yourself all the good news you can think of." — Thoreau
* You can take it with you
* Are you a "Secret Service Christian"?
* If God guides you, how can you go wrong?
* You didn't ask to be born, but neither did anybody else!
* What has God to do with what you're doing?
* Who needs your help today?
* You become what you think
* God calls you to a life of significant change
* It's still true — you must lose your life to find it!
* Are you getting your head straight? Jesus can help!
* What would an imaginative person do with your job?
* You are to love God and your neighbor as yourself
* "Cry to the Lord in your trouble — he will deliver you"
* If the Lord is your strength, you need fear none!
* Do you tell the world how wonderful God is?
* What on earth are you doing, for God's sake?
* God is in you for good!
* What makes you think you'll stay a Christian?
* The kingdom is yours if you're poor enough to receive it
* Give God your resentments as an offering!
* You have a great ministry in just listening!
* Everyone you meet is fighting some kind of battle!
* With your mind on him, God keeps you in perfect peace
* You find life by giving it for that greater than self
* Spend time on things that outlast time
* What you get from religion is up to you!
* God loves you! Get the sad look off!
* People see you behind your back as you look in front of them
* Look pleasant! In a way you are on candid camera!
* Let not your heart be troubled!
* Behave as though God were watching you!
* God comforts that you may be a comforter
* God wants not only to "convert" you but to invade you!

* Your whole life can sing to the glory of God!
* Can you stand for what you believe, on your principles?
* God wants to make a holy experiment of you!
* Are you an AWOL soldier of Christ?
* The Lord has need of you!
* Give God your will and he will show you life!
* Those who seek advice instead often want your praise
* Cast your anxieties on God, for he cares for you!
* If you're not living it, you don't have it yet!
* God so loved you that he gave his son for your everlasting life
* Do you believe that people are more important than things?
* God is big enough to take your hostility
* You can't solve your problem alone!
* Today: Give God your anxiety!
* If you want God only, you have all else besides!
* Today: Let God in on your whole life!
* A child of God gains nothing from self-downgrading
* Give God your fear right now!
* Your daily life reveals what you believe about yourself
* God's grace should be evident from your eyes
* You could change your tune!
* You could walk your worries off!
* You can't have inner peace by bouncing on it!
* What if you gain the whole world and lose your soul?
* Your big unsatisfied hunger is for God
* What gets your imagination gets you!
* Are your ideas of God the result of inner experience?
* Let your arithmetic be at its best when counting blessings
* Brighten the corner where you are!
* Are you happy with what you're doing for God?
* Lay up for yourself treasures in heaven
* Smile! God loves you!
* What soft spots are you guarding?
* Are you a neutral, gray Christian?
* Do your best with what you've got, where you are!
* Of what you wear your expression is the most important
* Blessed be this day to you and yours

* When you fight with your conscience and lose, you win!
* Not to insult yours, but there's a higher intelligence than yours
* This is the first day of the rest of your life!
* Your attitude rules your day!
* Do you major on minor things?
* Open the windows of your soul for spiritual ventilation!
* As you think in your heart, so are you!
* Honestly, now — what really guides and shapes your life?
* What you keep on thinking makes you what you are
* God can give you a track to run on!
* Running way from God keeps you exhausted!
* You form habits, then habits form you!
* It's hard to think of God when all you need is within reach
* What you ought to do you can do!
* Deal with the faults of others as gently as your own
* When you think you've achieved perfection, decline has set in!
* Are you living as if you were made for yourself?
* Would yours be a bought-off conscience?
* Where will you be 100 years from now?
* The secret of joy is to like to do what you have to do
* If you wrote your own epitaph, what would you say?
* Give your creative imagination to God!
* Do something to make the world better — improve yourself
* May you live all the days of your life!
* Do you have other gods before God?
* If this were judgment day, how would you do?
* You are made for eternity
* If you want to, you can have God for the rest of your life
* Is God showing you that you're phony?
* Who says you can't?
* What if your skin color would change instantly?
* Face to face with God you see clearly into your own heart
* You can be too careful!
* You trust your doctor — trust God!
* What is your vision for tomorrow?
* Pass over the faults of others, look first at yours

* Live as if this were your last day on earth
* Are you fun to live with?
* Is the world better because of you?
* You are entitled to love yourself properly
* Are you being good to God?
* When in your life were all conditions "go"?
* Lacking goods or title, who are you?
* Do you really love Jesus?
* Are you a one-person grievance committee?
* Be interested in the future — you'll spend your life there!
* These are good times if you know what to do with them!
* What are you accomplishing with your life?
* Take God's look at yourself
* Don't wait for the river to run out just before you cross!
* Life empty? Make sure you're putting something into it!
* Will the poor be sorry when you die?
* Spend your life for something that outlasts it
* Cross bridges in your imagination
* Why are you in this world?
* Don't make gods of your high moments
* Your very existence is a gift from God!
* The amazing love of God bids you grow tall in soul
* Your work is a portrait of yourself
* Are you blot or blessing?
* When you stop running, God can help you!
* You and God are a majority!
* Think how you can!
* If men speak ill of you, live so they're not believed
* In you is a continent of undiscovered talent
* Are you afraid to search yourself lest you find something good?

YOUTH

* Teenagers are like their parents were at their ages
* Youth need firm, understanding parents
* Teenage resolution: "Be patient with mother this year"
* Teenager: "I'm the kind my mother won't associate with"
* How can kids have good manners without seeing any?
* Hometown holds memories of you
* A childhood fault need not burden your life
* Better be square than move in the wrong circles!
* Jesus says, "Tune in and I'll turn you on and free you!"
* The earth is our all — let's not fumble the fall
* Money, fame, sex, drugs, put-ons will let you down!
* To kindle zeal in youth, give them things to die for!
* To influence youth — sell them on what they could become
* It's one thing to praise discipline, another to have it
* The mature can take blame which is not even theirs!

THE SEASONS

* Joy to the world — the Lord is come!
* Wise men still follow the star
* Christmas is tidings of comfort and joy
* At Christmas the shepherds glorified God — do you?
* "The dearest, truest Christmas is Christmas in the heart"
* Christmas is more than a visit to toyland
* Christmas can be a bitter day for mothers poor
* Christmas is Jesus' birthday!
* Is there room for him in your inn?
* Give Bibles for Christmas
* "What shall I give him?" Give him your heart!
* Live as if every day were Christmas
* Glory be to God on high and on earth, peace!
* What some call joy at Christmas is a pagan spree
* Scouting remembrance: "Today's brownie is tomorrow's cookie!"
* Some resolutions go in one year and out the other
* Good Friday is God's goodness overcoming man's badness
* Of the three who were crucified, two deserved it!
* I know that my Redeemer lives!
* Constant renewal comes from constant thanksgiving
* America, America! God shed his grace on thee!
* On Thanksgiving we celebrate our dependence
* The soul of America is torn between Christian and pagan
* "America is God's spoiled child." — Dr. Sam Shoemaker
* America is still the land of the free, the home of the brave!
* In God we trust
* In God we trust?
* America is living on blessings of its Christian past
* Life under the cross means relentless reformation
* What you give, give in love
* We cannot stand our dark side, so we repress it!
* "First they gave themselves"
* The kingdom of God is within you
* "A little brew will blur your view"

* Is the money we don't give to God taken in prices anyway?
* The oppressor needs to be liberated as well as the oppressed
* Mercy is love's supreme quality
* Medicine cabinet — home drug store without sandwiches
* Best things in life are free — worse are most expensive!
* Kindness goes a long way — maybe should stay at home some
* Lead a double life and finish in half the time
* Real friend — one who could tell you much but doesn't
* By the time you can stand for rights, arches are gone!
* Irritating — the one with less intelligence, more sense than you!

PEOPLE, FRIENDS

* A friend is a present you give yourself
* A friend knows all about you and still likes you!
* In your presence can people really be themselves?
* A friend you can count on when others count you out!
* A friend is one who lets you be fully yourself!
* "For a perfect brother, remain brotherless" — Italian saying
* Today — share your inward journey with others
* Psychiatrist: "I've never treated one who can laugh at self!"
* Of him to whom much has been given, much is required!
* "I inherited my friends from father, enemies I made myself!"
* Friendship doubles joy, divides grief!
* "God, make me ashamed of my vain self-centeredness"
* If you seek perfect friends, you'll never find them
* Drugs cut people off from people
* To empathize is to suffer with another
* See hypocrisy in others? Takes one to know one!
* Conflicts continue because we won't feel others' pain
* All people smile in the same language
* Friendship can only be bought by friendship
* Remind people of their worth
* Treat each person as if he's worth everything!
* Self-pity defeats more people than anything else!
* Today's kind of words bear fruit tomorrow!

BEING CRITICAL

* To the critical the whole world is at fault
* Criticism is a sword or sharp knife!
* Live a week in the world of one of whom you're critical!
* The critical hurt others because they've been hurt!
* "Judge not" even with silent judgment
* Criticism is usually a form of escape
* It is impossible to change others through criticism
* One word of criticism cancels ten of praise!
* When brushing teeth don't bother to sharpen tongue!
* The size of others' faults depends on how much they annoy you!
* Greatness is in enduring criticism without resentment
* Perfectionists are afraid of possible criticism!
* The criticism of the world shapes lives of most Christians!
* Destructive criticism is like killing frost
* He has the right to criticize who has the heart to help
* What you criticize in others, try to find in yourself!
* Like rain, criticism should encourage growth without destroying roots!
* "Walk a mile in his moccasins before judging." — Indian saying
* Criticism is destructive, felt or expressed

FORGIVENESS

* Character is shown by the criticism we forgive
* "Cheap grace" is forgiveness without repentance
* You forgive to the level that you permit forgiveness
* "Forgiveness ruptures ethics!" — Leander Keck
* Reunion of enemies comes through mutual forgiveness
* When forgiven, we are free to begin anew
* "Forget what is behind, reach for what is before!"
* When you dislike someone, do a loving thing for him!
* To understand is to pardon
* Better forget and smile than to remember and be upset!
* The sinful pharisees never felt that they were sinners!
* Only the admitted sinner feels God's forgiveness
* God's forgiveness marks our obligation "paid in full"!
* Real forgiveness handles real wrongs
* With forgiveness you're free to start over
* "I never forgive!" then may you never offend!
* Accept God's forgiveness and stop punishing yourself!
* God's forgiveness does not cancel moral law!
* Keep looking back and you find yourself going the wrong way
* The cost of God's forgiveness staggers — but it's worth it!
* The size of others' faults depends on how much they annoy you

CHURCH

* This house can make your home better!
* Worship is active response to God!
* This is the biggest church of its size in the world!
* Name a radiant Christian who doesn't go to church!
* An ember removed from the fire loses its glow!
* Ch??ch — what is missing?
* If absence makes the heart grow fonder, how some love church!
* Fight truth decay! Worship this Sunday!
* Worried about church surviving change? — offer currency!
* Don't judge a church by its worst examples
* The church needs to go where the people are!
* True worship is an experience of self-emptying
* The church also exists for those not in it!
* See you in church Sunday?
* The church is a body of seekers, not a museum of saints!
* The church needs to be a laboratory for change
* The church too easily domesticates its prophets!
* "Some churches are filled with 'retired Christians.'" — Ogilvie
* Little girl: "The church is the building with the plus on top!"
* No "local church" is only local!
* "Worship and social concern are Bible-based." — Cox
* Our altar is open for business all day!
* No church can possess or control the Holy Spirit!
* Go to church for the good you can do somebody else!
* The church needs to learn to stoop down
* The cross is the key to the church
* Worship is not for safety but adventure!
* "Good sermon! Every point hit somebody I know!"
* This church aims to be a vital center for Christian living
* This church is not embarrassed by the Holy Spirit!
* The "perfect church" wouldn't be after you joined it!
* Joining the church doesn't instantly make us God-centered
* "Church member" doesn't automatically mean "Christian"
* The church suffers from "bleeding heart-clean hands" syndrome

* The true church is above all nations, including U.S.A.!
* I was glad when they said, "Let us go to the House of the Lord!"

AFFIRMATIONS

* "Our souls are restless until they rest in thee"
* I know that my Redeemer lives!
* "I can do all things through Christ who strengthens me!"
* "In quietness and confidence will be my strength"
* With God, all things are possible
* "All things work together for good to those who love God"
* "The Lord is my shepherd — I shall not want"
* "I will never leave you nor forsake you." — Jesus
* "I give thanks to the Lord — his mercy endures forever!"
* "I taste and know that the Lord is good!"
* "I can depend on God's love and law!"
* God's forgiveness is the same yesterday, today, and forever
* "What I give away in God's name comes back blessed"

HOME, MARRIAGE

* You have to work your way through marriage
* Absence makes the heart go wander!
* Will your kids want a marriage just like yours?
* Divorce is hash made from domestic scraps
* Marriage should be a sacrament
* Love in the heart — music in the home
* "Faults are thick where love is thin" — Danish saying
* Men, help your wife burn the candle at at least one end!
* Marriages are usually happy — living together causes the trouble!
* She wrote, "Dear George, I hate you! Love, Alice"
* A real marriage is a God-made miracle!
* Sex is sinful only when used outside God's intention
* Living with others is tough, but who likes living alone?
* To live happily ever after, don't be after too much!
* God can make incompatible marriage compatible
* Judge: "I never had a divorce from a couple who prayed, read Bible"
* A happy marriage is the world's greatest bargain!
* Children not only comfort old age, they help reach it faster!
* Many convictions are only family hand-me-downs!
* This advice it pays to heed — don't plant more than wife can weed!
* A child is our second chance!
* A baby is a rivet in the bonds of matrimony
* Did you know that more businesses fail than marriages?
* It's a good marriage when both think they got the best of it
* New life, like charity, begins at home!
* "Season" your home life with love
* Success in marriage is not in finding but being the right person
* Nothing holds a family together like good behavior by parents
* A nation is built or destroyed child by child
* Best thing a man can do — help his wife correct his faults!
* We are what we are at home!
* Sick housewife's problem: "What do I stay home from?"

* Upset kids don't cry for "the principle of motherhood"
* Sex can be a god of pleasure holding people in bondage
* When mates take problems to God, accusations vanish
* Does your wife deserve a better husband? Vice versa?
* A contented husband helps with dishes without being asked
* Today's parent: "I said 'perhaps' and that's final!"
* Credit is a system of buying on the lay-awake plan
* Best way to compliment wife is frequently
* "Be it ever so humble, there's nobody home!"
* What's wrong with sex is what isn't right!
* Argument — longest distance between points of view
* Child: "Do we pray only at night for the cheaper rate?"
* Never do today what your wife can do tomorrow
* The best way to raise a child is to have two!
* Puppy love can lead to a dog's life!
* "Our argument closed when we admitted I was wrong"
* You can't be bitter all day and expect love at night
* Marriage is a partnership, not an ownership
* Sins of omission often break up a marriage
* Charity does begin at home!
* The best charity is the give-in kind!
* Every live family tree has some sap in it!
* It takes two good women to make a good husband
* Children need morals worse than critics
* The first Adam-splitting brought forth Eve
* Girls — a ring on the hand is worth two in the voice!
* If you could change three things about your mate, what are they?
* Let your arithmetic be at its best when counting blessings
* Patience — counting down when you feel like blasting off!
* At home live and help live!
* Keep a cemetery to bury the faults of your loved ones

WORRY, HATE, FEAR, SUFFERING, PRIDE

* Regret can be an awful waste of time!
* When you worry, you do not trust
* Try to recall what you worried about last week
* It's hard to worry and pray at the same time
* Worry kills more than work — more worry than work!
* Worry is the inability to let a difficulty go
* "Worry" is Anglo-Saxon for "choke" or "strangle"
* Christ can change your self-hate
* Hate is a prolonged form of suicide
* The deep sickening hatred of a grudge can kill you!
* In prayer, admit your hatred and God can heal
* Fear is faith in reverse
* Hurry indicates fear
* A brave person is scared but acts anyway
* Fear God and lose all your fears
* Fear is a form of consent
* God says to your fearful heart, "Be strong, fear not"
* Many go to the doctor when they are only afraid
* Fear knocked — faith answered. No one was there!
* Every day try to conquer a fear!
* Fear makes us hold onto problems too tightly
* Hate and fear are paralyzing viruses
* In the midst of plenty, some fear poverty
* Fear and hate destroy: Love and forgiveness heal
* God is greater than any of our problems
* If the Lord is your strength, you need fear none!
* Violence is fear turned inside out
* The tither is one who has no fear of the future
* "Courage is knowing what not to fear." — Socrates
* Suffering perfects and ennobles character
* Suffering fosters mercy, sympathy, understanding
* The ground is level before the cross
* God wants men great enough to be small enough to be used
* "The first product of self-knowledge is humility." — O'Connor

* Remember: Bethlehem too was a small place!
* When you know you have humility, you've lost it!
* When you think you've achieved perfection, decline has set in!
* A disciple kneels before the cross then gets under it!
* Neglect is a spiritual tool of temptation
* You can handle temptation without yielding to it!

SUCCEED, FAIL, STRUGGLE

* You're not a failure until satisfied with being one
* Defeat isn't so bitter if you don't swallow it
* Little can withstand a man who will conquer himself
* Failing is no disgrace but doing nothing is
* Success and failure are the harvest of habits
* Nothing conceits like success
* Wailing and failing are cousins
* For success: Find a need and fill it
* What's good in "Giving 'em something to be ashamed of"?
* No man is a failure who is enjoying life
* Success is what you're doing compared to your true potential
* Failure may come not from missing target but aiming too low
* Who are lost? Those who refuse God's love!
* Only they conquer who believe they can
* Stop running ... stop failing ... stand still and conquer
* Follow the crowd and quickly get lost in it!
* Cold feet? Maybe a sign soul is wearing out!
* A good loser is often a steady loser
* It takes struggle for good things to happen

OPTIMIST

* Is a pessimist one who lives with an optimist?
* Are you optimist or pessimist? Do you call signals "go-lights"?
* Optimists are usually happier than pessimists
* An optimist sees opportunity in difficulties

TRUTH

* The real truth will set you free
* The greatest thief is one who robs you of the truth
* Guilt: truth ache
* Truth sometimes seems intolerant
* "Honesty" can be brutal
* The truth usually sounds dogmatic
* "Telling the honest truth" means bringing up something nasty
* The cornerstone of Christian faith is truth, not tolerance
* The knowledge of heart exceeds that of the mind
* The truths of the Spirit are higher than science's
* When perfect truth comes, life takes on new meaning
* Stretch the truth and it snaps back!
* Disciples know the truth which makes us true
* When we quarrel some truth is always lost
* There is a truth that we can know within ourselves

ENTHUSIASM

* Keep the fires of enthusiasm burning under your goals
* To lose enthusiasm is to go bankrupt
* Give up enthusiasm and wrinkles come in your soul
* Enthusiasm is the spice of life
* Enthusiasm changes people
* "None is so old as the one who's outlived enthusiasm." — Thoreau
* Enthusiasm means "God in you" or "Full of God"
* "Enthusiasm is faith set on fire." — George Adams
* Lost enthusiasm wrinkles the soul

HAPPINESS, JOY

* Happiness is feeling joy in life's worth
* Joy is an inside job
* Don't consume happiness without producing some
* It is more joyful to give than to receive
* "The soul's highest duty is to be of good cheer." — Emerson
* "Happy ever after" is for those who work at it
* Real Christianity is a new, courageous, joyful life
* Sons of God have peace, joy, and confidence
* Unhappiness can be a bad habit
* Unhappiness comes from a mix of ingratitude and fear
* The unhappy are usually negative
* Your whole life can sing to the glory of God!
* Happiness is making bouquets of flowers within reach
* Without meaning, the search for happiness is dead
* Happiness is not a station — it's a way
* The way to be happy is to make others happy
* Happiness is the conviction that we are loved
* Obedience to God produces joy
* Six-year-old: "I want to be a professor of happiness"
* True happiness cannot come from fleeting pleasures
* The greatest joy is fellowship with God
* Joy is a by-product of seeking God
* Counterfeit joy is at a price of a few beers
* Happiness comes little by seeking it
* For true happiness: Do a kindness every day
* Happiness is health, ideals, freedom to carry them out
* Happiness is more interests than assets

KINDNESS

* Kindness converts more people than learning
* Today's kind words may bear fruit tomorrow
* Gratitude is the most exquisite form of courtesy
* Be kind one to another — tenderhearted, forgiving
* Kindness makes friends of enemies
* Kindness takes you by the hand, doesn't care where you've been
* Kindness is sunshine after the storm
* Today: Send encouraging thoughts to others

FREE

* God's gift of free-will is a "do-it-yourself" kit
* Christ gives you freedom not to drink
* Man is the freest thing on earth
* Freedom is God's great risk
* Free men believe in the other's freedom
* Violence discredits the ideal of freedom
* Denying freedom to another is a step to losing your own
* To get freedom's blessings we must work to support it
* "Free" is not the same as "free and easy"
* A world of freedom requires free choice of good and evil
* The best things in life are not so much free as unexpected
* Today's freedom needs Christ's discipline
* Disciples know the truth which makes us free
* When forgiven, we are free to begin anew
* We don't get free when we confess the wrong sin!
* When free from guilt, we have nothing to conceal
* Stop trying to escape from the universe!